WLA Folios: Body

ISBN-13: 978-0-692-06546-4

Cover: Sculpture by Gina Herrera. Design by William Newmiller

TABLE OF CONTENTS

JESSE GOOLSBY & KATIE WITT

EDITORS, *WLA FOLIOS*

At *War, Literature & the Arts*, we celebrate work that expands and challenges our perception of peace, conflict, being, and presence, well beyond traditional and expected notions of war and repose.

For the 2018 edition of *WLA Folios*, a curated and themed issue of *War, Literature & the Arts*, we chose the subject of Body. Thirteen distinguished contributors were asked to consider the body, and we're thrilled to share the compelling and beautiful work featured here.

We hope you enjoy *WLA Folios: Body*.

ANGELA MORALES

Mammalian

When I was sixteen-years old and a sophomore in high school, my cousin Kristy, age eighteen, selected me to be her birthing "coach." She'd tested positive on the home pregnancy test, gotten dumped by her twenty-three-year old boyfriend, and against the advice of almost everyone, had decided to raise the baby on her own. As her birthing coach, I would fail miserably, since I possessed neither a commanding presence nor faith in the Lamaze philosophy—exercises, which, frankly, I thought were embarrassing and stupid. I could barely force myself to lead Kristy through the "Hee-Hee-Ha-Ha" breathing exercises which the Lamaze teacher insisted would help my partner to manage her pain, nor could I flutter my fingertips across her back or arms, a technique which our bandanna-wearing, ruddy cheeked teacher called "effleurage" and then assured us ("us" being husbands and boyfriends) that the distraction of a light touch could be, not only *romantic*, but would help our partners (our partners being wives and girlfriends) to remain calm and focused. Not a "touchy" person by nature, my hands must have felt unsettling and possibly irritating to Kristy, as it pained me to trace little circles on her arm or to massage her lower back. Though we'd practically grown up together, and I knew her better than just about anybody, I could be aloof and unexpressive, even with the people whom I loved the most.

In Grandma Ruth's stacks of *National Geographic*, I'd run across photographs of indigenous women giving birth—maybe Yanomami in the rainforest or Mayan women, always the laboring woman grimacing and biting down on a rag as she squatted naked or barely clothed and leaned against a tree or another woman. Another woman always attended—sometimes a whole team of women—mothers, sisters, aunties, and even elders who sat vigil nearby, chanting and praying and burning incense, all of them participating in some kind of mass hallucination that would help ease the baby from eternal darkness and into the light of day.

Then, there we were—eighteen and sixteen-years-old—alone in a windowless, sterile hospital room, armed only with a Styrofoam cup filled with ice chips, not a tree or river or star in sight. Cut off from the natural world and any community of women, we stared at each other in a panic. Where was our oak tree? Would the sound of a river have eased her pain? Where were the elders? Like an animal caught in a trap, Kristy began to lose her mind, and all I could do was gawk at her, stunned by nature's merciless grip. That day I vowed never to get knocked-up, never to allow my body to become overtaken by whatever mysterious pleasures might result in a million tadpoles swimming upstream into *my* uterus.

Sitting on the floor next to her hospital bed and wearing my paper booties, I leaned against the wall, closed my eyes, and resigned myself to failure. I could not guide my poor cousin in any way. I decided that all I could do was sit beside her—another body in the room. Finally, after seventeen or eighteen hours of watching my cousin writhe in agony, the nurses appeared, all business, methodically positioning a surgical lamp over the bed, raising the metal stirrups, and ordering this teenage Jane Doe, this random eighteen-year-old unmarried girl to breathe. *Breathe*!

After a while of this—of nurses scolding Kristy and demanding that she push harder, and Kristy shrieking to them that they could all go to hell—there, suddenly, appeared a baby—wriggling and red, followed by a great splash of blood and amniotic fluid that filled the room with the overpowering smell of iron. I couldn't take my eyes off the big, squirming creature that, indeed, appeared to have catapulted from some unknown darkness and into the light of the world. That one young female body could produce an offspring so large and vociferous, and with such violence! And that through an opening so small could appear another human being! I swooned (literally) at the thought of it. Dizzy and nauseous, I backed up against the wall and sank to the floor as the glistening placenta slid onto a metal tray and the baby exercised her new lungs. I sat there like that, numbed, until the nurses told me that I needed to pick myself up and get out of the way.

Fat women are often made to feel ugly, lesser than, sloppy, undisciplined, and unsexy, but young children generally do not judge the worth of a woman or the affection they feel for her based on her body size, especially if those children already love large women, i.e. their mothers or aunties or grandmothers, women who have nurtured them, comforted them, fed them, told them stories. To children, a woman's body size is never part of the equation that totals her overall goodness or worth and it rarely occurs to those children that anyone would find such generous bodies unattractive and repellent. It never occurs to those children that those very same women might look in the mirror with self-loathing and a longing to be less than, to be smaller, to reduce themselves. Children enjoy a large woman's body—soft, strong arms that gently crush them against wide-soft bellies, a safe place where they can feel the warmth and generosity of a human body.

My mother, an average-sized woman with a body that produced five healthy babies, rarely hid her naked body from her children, each morning, dressing with her bedroom door wide open. I recall standing before her, talking to her about whatever random topic, as she perfumed, oiled, shaved, or powdered her body, and examined herself in the mirror, bending this way and that way, peering at her neck, maybe plucking her eyebrows, filing her nails. My mother's breasts were not small and perky like the women in *Charlie's Angels*; my mother's breasts were large and heavy and laced with blue veins. Her belly and thighs were pale and soft as dough, and because I'd seen her body my whole life, it never occurred to me that her body should be different somehow—thinner, more muscular, hidden away. My mother's naked body looked to me the way a body *should* look. Sometimes to entertain us, she'd perform a kind of Polynesian dance in her underwear that would get her fat jiggling all at once, the loose flesh and her thighs and belly all wobbly and out of control, like her fat had gone crazy. Watching her, we nearly busted a gut, as she liked to say. Women's bodies can be hilarious. Nobody talks much about that.

Three days after giving birth to my son, I thought that I was dying. My arms felt tingly, my chest throbbed and burned, and I felt panicky. Of course, my symptoms were part of the normal lactation process. Women, for the first few days post-partum, produce only small amounts of a thick substance called colostrum, easily digestible for the newborn and rich in immunoglobulin A and leukocytes, all good for fighting infection. In the first few days, new mothers who nurse their babies often fret over whether the baby is getting any nutrients at all. But, normally, if all goes well, in the span of a few hours, the "mature" milk floods in, and the baby will have hit the jackpot. When the floodgates opened in my body, in the span of an hour or two, my breasts ballooned to ridiculous proportions and became absurdly round. Engorged. Inflated. Nature had claimed me.

Part A: my breasts had become *milk storage vessels.* I had read about lactation, but reading does not equal experiencing.

Part B: the milk would need to get *out* once it had come in. Thus, feeding the baby became my promise to him, and I set myself on a mission to fulfill that promise. Once I figured out how to sit, how to position the baby with a pillow under his head, how to relax, how to sip a cold drink, how to close my eyes, take a deep breath, and pray for "release"—a mild cramping would occur and then a steady, miraculous flow. Human milk. An elixir, a panacea, the baby slept soundly, and day-by-day, grew plumper, more alert, and happier.

Thus, I allowed nature to claim me. I surrendered. Sitting in this chair or that chair, gazing out this window or that window, looking at this tree or that tree, I thought about all sorts of things and nothing at all. I watched a blue jay hopping around on the potato vine. I studied a spider rappelling down her strand of silk; I told myself that if I did nothing else within the span of a day except *feed the baby*, I would have done my job like any resilient mammal minding her instincts. My consciousness simultaneously dimmed and expanded. Those hours and hours and hours of feeding the baby I let my thoughts roll on by: the shape of nipples, both plastic and real, pacifiers, the cream layer atop milk, wet nurses, silicone implants, starving babies, twin orbs, rivers flowing, rivers blocked, serrated teeth, the sun and the moon.

My body and my mind split up briefly when I was nine years old and had fallen off my bike and hit my head on the curb. I wasn't wearing a helmet, and I don't recall the accident, but I do recall the distinct sensation of emerging from a fog while sitting in the emergency room. It was as though my mind had been put inside another body and suddenly my consciousness had flickered back on as if someone had plugged me in. I saw my feet hanging limply from the chair. My hands appeared big and useless. My face felt throbby and swollen. Strangers talked at me, a crowd of faces, all of them peering down at me and pursuing nonsensical questions, and I didn't know the answers. I did not know what they expected of me. Name? Age? I had no clue. President of the United States? I did not know if a president was a type of bird or a cat or a food that you ate for dinner. My brain recognized some words but not others. The word "president" sounded as foreign to me as Swahili. United States: A blur of syllables. My brain slipped deeper into its cave like a mollusk recoiling into its shell while my body remained in the room. Somewhere between brain and body, the "I" remained, abandoned by both.

Did amnesia allow one girl to walk away and another girl to step in? How does one know when one regains consciousness, whether *you* are the same you who lost consciousness? Who was that girl staring at the doctors with her vacant expression? That girl, like a lighthouse keeper, tended my body as the other girl slipped away.

Neurologists say that a head injury leaves all kinds of mysteries, and the complete effects to any one brain may never be known. What exactly happened to my brain upon impact with the curb on Country Club Drive that day in 1976 might be unknown forever, secrets lost in stardust. As my cauliflower-brain banged around in its skull case, shaken up in its bath of cerebral-spinal fluid, did the injury scare away my then-self and make way for a new self? Did it deaden certain control towers and awaken others, like the language area, the cerebral cortex? Certainly, the injury left me confused, but perhaps with letters and words all scrambled up but closer to the surface for easier access in some future life.

When we say "the body," it sounds like we might be referring to a murder scene. "The body was found partially clothed and floating in the river," said the detective. It's like when a person dies, they cease to be a person and are reduced to the flesh, to the body form. If the person is still alive, we look for the person. If the person is thought to be dead, we look for the body.

"She has a nice body," someone might say, as if that body is not something exactly representing her –not her, but something she has. One might say, "She has a nice dog," in a similar fashion. A body can be dead or alive, but it does not necessarily equal the sum of the person.

The Mayans tossed the bodies of sacrificial children into massive cenotes in the rainforest of the Yucatan. You might shout into a cenote and not hear an echo; your voice would disappear down into the earth, into a hole so deep that birds can fly around inside it. What became of those tiny bodies as they smashed against the water so far below, scarcely making a sound? Their bodies decomposed in silence over the centuries, bones dissolving, bodies absorbing into the deepest of rivers, cell by cell.

We might find it necessary to destroy a body before it begins. If the developing body is connected to our bodies, we sometimes feel that the new body will require more life than we are able to give. We imagine its pinky-nail sized existence, a transparent clump of cells buried deep inside our own spongy centers, a pulsating quasar of possibilities, a faint set of signals sent from another galaxy—the galaxy of us, and the signals keep getting stronger. We want to trust that our bodies will know the instincts of animals and that we can numb our chattering minds—that loathsome lump of cream cheese that sits in our skulls, that worries for our bodies, questions our choices, berates us, solves riddles, shows us, in dreams and flashes, our failures.

If only, if only, if only we could silence our brains, the thing that is "us" and let the body swell, let this new body grow, not think or question, but simply Be. When a new body begins, when we cannot sustain it, it's as though we are caught in a net.

Diagnosed with chronic Lyme Disease, I had just begun a monthlong round of I.V. antibiotics when a new body began inside my body. I did not have the strength to imagine my own future much less the literal strength to carry this new body inside my sick body. My joints had deteriorated. My heart fluttered. I could barely carry a bag of groceries. I could barely make a peanut butter and jelly sandwich for my living child. "A child is a blessing," Dr. Reddy said. I wanted to ignore my brain. I wanted to close my eyes and allow my body to bloom like a flower. I tried. I failed. Ultimately, I chose my body over the new body. At the clinic I was warned that my decision might haunt me forever and that I would carry with me a profound, unshakable guilt and sadness. Confession: I felt [mostly] relief. I suppose one could say that I was "pro-life." My life.

In the hospital emergency exam room, the intake nurse asks Patrick, my husband, to leave the room. "I'd like to speak to your wife alone," she says, giving him a sidelong glance as he slips out the door. To me, she says, "Has your husband hit you or hurt you or threatened you?" I am clutching my abdomen, rocking away my pain, with what will turn out to be an infected gallbladder; I am caught off guard.

"Has he *what*?" I say, awakening from my pain-trance.

"Has you husband hurt or threatened you tonight?" she repeats, with sharp flashing eyes and a no-nonsense expression.

"No," I say. "Never." I expect her to soften her tone, that she'll laugh and say, "Yeah, Sorry. We're required to ask." But she does not soften. She continues to search my face giving me time to change my answer. I wonder if this line of questioning is standard or whether she had suspected abuse because of Patrick's dour expression, his crossed arms, because every single minute of every single day, men slam their fists into their wives' bodies, their girlfriends, their daughters (and yes, women do it, too. And, yes, there are abused men, but most cases involve men believing that a woman's body belongs to them).

You are my wife; therefore, I can.

My husband's fists have never slammed into my body; my husband's hands are healing and gentle. (I learned early-on how to evaluate a man's hands—my father taught me when to duck and to memorize the contours of knuckles as they collided with my mother's arm or leg or cheek).

But as the nurse searches my eyes, the reminder of this everyday truth intensifies my pain. I clutch my abdomen and begin to cry. The pain is unbearable, and I suspect the nurse does not believe me. How could I explain to her, and how could I explain to myself, that her questions have transformed my mundane gallbladder pain into a lightning-strike of all the pain of all the women in all the world who have ever felt a fist slam into their bellies, the fist of someone who supposedly loves them.

One day when the baby was about a year old, I was busy making dinner, rushing around the kitchen in a cloud of steam—chopping vegetables, sautéing, boiling, whatever. He had reached the age of escape-artist, expert-climber, adept at squeezing into cabinets, at demolishing the living room by throwing every object he could find into a massive heap in the middle of the room, like Roy's mad sculpture of Devil's Tower in *Close Encounters of the Third Kind.*

Sometimes I would give the baby the telephone to play with. I'd unplug it and let him push the buttons and puzzle over the coiled rubber cord. But this night, in a rush, I handed him the phone, forgetting to unplug it. He played with it for a few minutes, and I finished cooking and scooped him up for his bath. Just as I was lowering my chubby boy into the bath water, someone's fists began pounding on the front door. No neighbor or kid selling candy bars had ever knocked like that. I scooped him back up, wrapped him in a towel, and peered around the hallway with a view to the glass-paneled front door. Under the porch light stood a police officer, a stocky black man with a gleaming, brass badge. He held a night stick in one hand and kept the other hand positioned over his gun.

Cautiously, I opened the door.

"You called 9-1-1," he said quietly, leaning in close.

Then it dawned on me. "Oh my God!" I said, immediately realizing what had happened. I clapped my hand across my mouth. "I'm so sorry," I said. "The baby…he was playing with the phone!"

I expected this police officer to give me a stern lecture about letting babies play with phones. A lecture about wasting taxpayers' money. About diverting police officers from legitimate calls. About how 9-1-1 wasn't a joke.

But he kept staring into the house, eyes scanning the living room, the dining room, as far as he could see.

"You sure you're ok?" he said, his eyes searching mine.

"I'm fine," I said, again, expecting his eyes to soften, for him to say, "Well, we just have to make sure." But his eyes did not soften, nor did he give me a lecture.

"Mind if I look around?" he said quietly.

"Sure," I said, backing away from the door to let him pass. Briefly, I was annoyed that he didn't believe me. For a minute I felt that he was overstepping his boundaries. Holding his holster with one hand, his night stick with the other, he strutted from end to end of the house, peering into the bedroom, into the closets, his heavy step firm and steadfast.

When he returned, he said, "I had to make sure someone wasn't hiding in the bedroom or that someone wasn't holding you hostage. Sorry about that."

"Hostage? Really? Well…thank you," I said. I mean, here was this man who had arrived to protect me when I did not even need protecting. Here was this man saving me from a hypothetical hostage-taker, a husband who'd punched a wall, my theoretical abusive husband who'd promised to choke me or stab me if I'd said one word.

"I'm really sorry about this," I said again, jostling my big fat baby.

"It's okay, it's okay," he said, "It happens. Glad you're safe."

Leo and I watched him walk down the concrete path back to his police car. Again, I thought of the ways that men brutalize women, the ways that people brutalize children, the ways that police brutalize other men. But for that one moment, I felt thankful for this one man who would have protected me had I needed protecting.

ANGELA MORALES, a graduate of the University of Iowa's nonfiction writing program, is the author of *The Girls in My Town*, a collection of personal essays. Her work has appeared in *Best American Essays 2013*, *Harvard Review*, *The Southern Review*, *The Southwest Review*, *The Los Angeles Review*, *Arts and Letters*, *The Baltimore Review*, *The Pinch*, *Hobart*, *River Teeth*, *Under the Sun*, *and Puerto del Sol*, *and The Indianola Review*. She is the winner of the River Teeth Book Prize, 2014, and is a MacDowell Fellow. Her book is the 2017 winner of the PEN Diamonstein-Spielvogel Award for the Art of the Essay. Currently she teaches composition and creative writing at Glendale Community College and is working on her second collection of essays.

DUNYA MIKHAIL

Plastic Death

In my childhood
in Baghdad
we played dead:
we killed each other
with plastic weapons.
We lay on the floor,
still as corpses,
for a minute
or two.
Then one of us laughed,
exposing our plastic death,
we held each other
as the dying might
life itself, but rose
to play another game.
The years turn over like lotto numbers,
and Baghdad recedes
with our childhoods
into exile.
From afar, we see children
who look like we did.

They kill each other,
lie motionless
on the floor.
But none of them laugh
or hold life
and rise.

DUNYA MIKHAIL is an Iraqi-American poet. Her books include *The Beekeeper: Rescuing the Stolen Women of Iraq, The Iraqi Nights*, *Diary of A Wave Outside the Sea*, and *The War Works Hard.* Her honors include the Kresge Fellowship, Arab American Book Award, and UN Human Rights Award for Freedom of Writing. She currently works as an Arabic special lecturer at Oakland University in Michigan. She has a BA from the University of Baghdad and an MA from Wayne State University. Mikhail is the co-founder of Mesopotamian Forum for Art and Culture in Michigan.

TOM PIAZZA

IED

You could not keep it all in mind at once. Say, how cool it was, walking down early morning Broadway before the sun rose high enough to warm the storefronts and dry the hosed-down sidewalks. The cars and taxis waiting at the lights, the three men with the moustaches shouting and carrying a man's body across a street littered with chunks of masonry, steel reinforcement rods sticking out like grey bones, twisted, and hazy with dust from yet another collapsed house and yet another car vomiting its black smoke in tumbling rolls that float away on the light breeze. Or say the array of fabulous smoked fish laid out on the ice banks behind the shiny glass in the refrigerator cases at Zabar's, and below on the narrow shelf the jars of caviar arranged to highlight the contrasting label colors. Cool morning haze still clings to the chained bay waters liberty south of Battery Park, the beckoning statue in the distance raising her torch, our torch, their torch, to the morning ocean glare and seagulls while the cranes clank and the tractors pull and the bulldozers roll on their tank treads at the site, the hole, the wound still emitting all those glass microparticles and metallic dust, while the turquoise ceramic tile is cool in the shadow of the alley behind the mosque as a cart passes what is left of the east wall of the school that was built only five years ago, covered now with spray-painted anguish letters... And the grey-haired man with trousers going thready draws too close, bad teeth and worse breath, asking, where is security, where is security Americans promised? Or the large round tables being set up just inside the stone park walls at 63rd Street for the Central Park Zoo's annual "Spring Fling," or maybe it's the "Zoo To-Do," the white table cloths and flowers and the staff in black slacks, white shirts, and black bowties—does this seem random yet?—and there is a man with his back on fire, his clothes blown off, his hair, too, walking with his back on fire, a look of urgency in his eyes as he walks through the smoking chunks of debris and body parts, this was his last view of the world, do you understand? Think of the eggs put on to boil and forgotten and the return, hours later, to find a foot of thick smoke hugging the ceiling and in the kitchen flecks of egg all over the walls and ceiling, no water left in the pan, one fragment of egg in its shell, rocking back and forth, and the man on fire finally caves in and lies on his back with his eyes still open, rocking slightly back and forth looking up at his God and what did God see, looking down at him? Tell me what did God think, if you're so fucking smart...

the wisdom of the past and the faith of the future, a future that just

[text removed]

[flash; black smoke]

I will have the tournedos, thank you.

(switch channels)

Eggs, bacon, coffee cans, phone jacks, piles of clothes... You can't look without going blind, without the protective lenses in the narrative frames, the lockstep of consequence and time... Narrative is original sin; where is there an end of it? Talk to me, you motherfucker, or I will break your fucking jaw so you can't talk. The pure products of America go crazy. Those are lemon tarts; they are exquisite... I'm sorry, I had the card somewhere here in my pocket... A sneaker, a smoldering tire, Cantor Fitzgerald stationery, charred around the edges, fluttering down over Brooklyn Heights like tickertape in the golden air... Old poems in a box, used kerchiefs, the best bagels, that expensive purse, the conversation at NOHO Star after the Pasolini screening, a fish lunging and tearing at the white carcass floating belly-up, the fuselage, dancing with the brandished rifle overhead, charred body parts hanging from the bridge, such an achievement, it's marvelous to have such talent, but was that three months later, before or after the delicious tandoori chicken we had at the place on Second Street, the red marinade charred and so tasty... The frame blows apart, breaks the bottle in the climate-controlled cellar—a wine is a narrative—they smash the bottles, they trample the vintage...

And you, Great Leader, want assent, consent, the shared narrative which is no narrative at all, the great transcendent narrative of God's unchanging will, not subject to time except that the snake was in God's employ... Nothing happens in Paradise, and nothing happens in Hell, either, and what motive moves secretly out there beyond the margin, beyond the page, the screen, unseen and gradual; what if the bomb goes off in your narrative, kicks over your ant hill in the name of reality, in the name of truth, in the name of some God who promises to absolve you of this hideous lockstep... Wouldn't you scramble to rebuild it? Who could ever blame you?

TOM PIAZZA is the author of twelve books of fiction and nonfiction, including the novels *A Free State* and *City Of Refuge*, the post-Katrina manifesto *Why New Orleans Matters*, and the essay collection *Devil Sent The Rain*. He was a principal writer for the innovative HBO drama series *TREME*, and the winner of a Grammy Award for his album notes to *Martin Scorsese Presents The Blues: A Musical Journey*. He lives in New Orleans.

DAVID CHRISINGER

In the Shadow of an Unanswered Question

My grandfather died on a Sunday. His name was Harold Chrisinger—his friends called him "Hod." He was a rough-hewn man, undereducated and overburdened, who fought in the Second World War and came home a drunk. He didn't want to fight. Some think that's why he knocked up my grandmother before either one of them could finish high school. Maybe they wouldn't need a man with a baby on the way. The draft board took him anyway, and by the time his daughter was born, in the early fall of 1944, he was training for war. By the time he turned 19, he was on the island of Okinawa, fighting in the longest and deadliest battle of the Pacific Theater. He didn't like to talk about his war. He never spoke a word of it to me, and my father remembers only a handful of stories, fragments really.

I heard from my father's older brother once that when my grandfather was a younger man, when he still hung around some of the other veterans in town, he would talk. Only to other veterans, though. Usually around the John Deere tractor repair shop my grandfather ran with his father. My uncle would hang around there sometimes when he was little and listen in when the other fellas started telling their stories. He remembers Hod mostly listening while he turned wrenches and checked fluids, sometimes scoffing or rolling his eyes at the stories he heard. If someone pressed him to share something about the war, he would look up from whatever motor he was working on and tell them about the Shermans he was trained to drive, what a bitch they were to steer. He'd laugh about the sergeant he met at the processing center at Fort Sheridan, just north of Chicago. He'd found out my grandfather grew up on a farm and knew how to drive a tractor. *If you can drive a tractor,* he'd said, *you can drive a tank.* Round peg. Round hole. Sometimes he'd say that his tank company had been nearly wiped out in some disastrous battle no one back home had ever heard about, that the mission was doomed from the beginning. Incompetent officers, he'd say as he wiped the sweat from his brow with the back of his grease-stained hand. The other vets would nod in commiseration.

There was one story he didn't mind telling his family. Sometimes, when the mood struck, he would talk about a captain he admired who would sit with my grandfather and the other men in the company at night, just before the mortars started thundering down around them, and check to make sure they had everything they needed. That's what a *real* leader looks like, he'd say. Not like his lieutenant. He hated his lieutenant, mostly because he'd threatened to shoot my grandfather once, late in the battle, while they were tasked with mopping up the last of the Japanese resistance on the island. The company was patrolling somewhere in the hills on the northern half of the island, and my grandfather discovered a young, unarmed Japanese soldier hiding in the brush. The lieutenant thought my grandfather had been too gentle with the prisoner, so he chewed my grandfather's ass and threatened to shoot him if he didn't start treating the enemy like the treacherous bastards they were. *That Jap was just a scared kid, like me,* my grandfather would say.

I was only fourteen-years-old when my grandfather passed. At that time, I hadn't heard any of these stories about him. I didn't know where he had served or what he had done. I only found those things later, after I began my investigation. All I knew was that he fought and that he came home a changed man. That's what everyone said. In the years after the war, he did things and said things—terrible things. Things no husband or father should ever do or say. Things that people avoided talking about because he was a war hero. But I didn't know what those things were exactly. My father's family didn't like to talk about those things. My father hated being asked questions. Most of what I learned about my grandfather when I was a teenager, I learned from my mother. She would tell me about all the childhood trauma my father had survived. Looking back, I think she wanted me to better understand why my father had a tendency to be emotionally distant, numb even. The one story that's stuck with me after all these years is the one about the night my grandmother rolled her eyes to something cruel my grandfather said to her at the dinner table. Instead of apologizing, my grandfather flew into a fit of rage, grabbed her by the hair in front of my father and his young siblings, dragged her into the bathroom, and stuck her head face first into the toilet. After he was finished, he returned to the dinner table—my grandmother sobbing in a ball on the bathroom floor—and continued eating his porkchop and baked potato as if nothing happened.

On the day before my grandfather was slated to be buried, the nondescript funeral home in Hixton, Wisconsin that prepared his body hosted a wake in the early evening. As my father and I approached the front door of the home, about an hour before the wake was supposed to begin, a late summer breeze whistled through the green-leafed trees that lined the parking lot. As we entered the front entryway, a flowery fragrance overpowered the scent of freshly cut grass that dominated the outside air. As my father and I entered the parlor with its gold-yellow walls and dimly lit wall sconces, we found my grandfather's silver casket open on the upper half and positioned as far from the door as possible. Stands of flowers flanked each end of the casket, and a small oak table with a folded American flag and a black and white photo of my grandfather in his tan service uniform standing next to my grandmother stood sentry near the foot. The funeral director was nowhere to be found, so my father ducked out to locate him. Left alone with my grandfather, I felt this strange compulsion to see his body up close. I'd seen a handful of dead deer and other animals I'd hunted in the woods of central Wisconsin, but I'd never seen the lifeless body of someone I knew.

As I cautiously approached the casket, like a hunter stalking through the forest, my tan corduroy pants swished with each step. This was my first funeral, and I had no black pants or shirts. The best I could muster was a maroon short-sleeved button-up and tan pants. When I reached the foot of the casket, I looked at the framed photo of my grandparents then peered over the edge of the casket, suddenly afraid I might somehow disturb the presentation. The first thing I noticed, after pushing my glasses up higher on my nose, was how healthy my grandfather looked compared to the last time I'd seen him alive. That time he was lying in a hospital bed, trapped beneath a tangle of cords and hoses. His body was swollen, and the air was heavy with August humidity and smelled of disinfectant.

He had been near death when my father found him in the one-room shack he called home. That day, my father discovered my grandfather hunched over his small, Formica-topped table, legs spread wide, his bloated gut resting between his thighs and bulging out of his dirty overalls. His breathing was labored; his eyes bulged out of his head. The blood vessels in his nose had mostly popped, leaving red and purple scratch-like streaks flowing over his nose and under his eyes. I doubt he had been expecting company, for if he had, he probably would have made sure he wouldn't get caught with a half empty bottle of black berry brandy and a garbage can full of crushed Old Style cans. The year before, the doctors at the VA told my father that if my grandfather didn't stop drinking, he'd soon be dead. And it wouldn't be quick or painless, either. Cirrhosis of the liver kills you slowly. My grandfather's blood pressure was way too high, the doctors said, and none of the medication they tried was having much of an effect. He was also losing excretory function. My father didn't know what that was and at the time didn't have the wherewithal to ask for clarification. Plus, there was the massive ascites—the extreme bloating of the belly—and the variceal hemorrhages. And the hepatic encephalopathy and renal impairment. That's what you get, the doctors said, after nearly six decades of alcoholism.

As my father sped to the hospital with my grandfather beached in the backseat of the four-door sedan he was driving, my father tried to keep my grandfather awake and talking. They talked about the weather and how the hay was ready for the third harvest of the year. This was the busy time of the year for my grandfather when he was still working. For four decades, he had been known as the best combine mechanic in three counties. It was the only thing he was ever good at.

At his father's hospital bedside, my father wanted to say something—anything. He would have liked to say good bye and that he forgave him for all the hurt and anguish he put the family through, but my father couldn't find the words. The shame was still too raw, the smell too intense. He wasn't even dead yet, but my grandfather had begun to rot. Instead of talking, my father stood and stared at this man who had scared and tormented him for so long, who was now nothing more than a weak, dying old man. He looked at his face, the wisps of hair on the top of his head and the silver three-day-old stubble that covered his chin and cheeks. He saw himself. Unlike the rest of his siblings, my father couldn't bring himself to forgive or to even hope that he and his father were going to get another chance, in some other place, at some other time, to discover who the other was. He didn't understand his father, and his father didn't understand him, and there was nothing he could say in those last few hours to change that.

Lying in his casket, my grandfather looked peaceful and calm—a testament to the funeral director's skill. The caked-on makeup covered up the evidence of the broken blood vessels, and a clean shave paired with the desiccation that occurs at death left him looking square-jawed and resolute. His eyes and mouth were closed, and his upper body was dressed in a white, short-sleeved, button-up shirt long out of style.

I realized as I came up next to him that I had never really studied his face before. In the summertime, when my father would take us along for our annual visit with Grandpa Hod, I was always to nervous to look at him. He scared me. After we'd arrive, my brother, mother, and I would stand in the tall, un-mowed grass in my grandfather's front yard as my father knocked on the door and went inside to see if his father was even still alive. My father feared for years that it would take weeks for someone to discover if my grandfather was dead. He had no friends. No telephone. Once inside his house, we would line up as a family, from tallest to shortest, and try not to stick to anything while my father chit-chatted with my grandfather. The tension exhausted me.

Looking at his face now for the first time I felt alone with him and scared of what his body might feel like. I pictured him opening his eyes, smiling at me, like this was all a big practical joke. After turning to see whether anyone had entered the parlor without me realizing it, I turned back to my grandfather and reached out a shaking hand. I first poked his chest, just under the collar bone. There was no more elasticity to his skin. Not like when you poke the jelly-like body of a deer you've just shot to make sure it's really dead. He was more rock than flesh. Feeling emboldened, I placed my left hand on his chest, near where his heart once beat. It was only for a moment. Then I heard a rustling behind me and quickly stuffed both my hands into my pockets. I kept looking at my grandfather's face, pretending I hadn't just felt him up, as my father approached from behind and to my left. He placed his right hand on my left shoulder and stared inside the casket with me.

The dark, yellowy complexion of my grandfather's face made it seem as if it had been sculpted in wax. I realize now, seventeen years later, that it was this waxiness that prevented any sort of feeling of intimacy, not that there ever had been any of that before he died. I don't remember crying at all that day. Maybe because I was no longer looking at my grandfather, but something that resembled him. A shell that was once a body. Maybe because I never really knew him. Maybe because he never wanted to be known. As far as I was concerned, he was but a couple of pictures and a handful of fragmented stories. It's hard to mourn such an abstraction.

When I was young, I didn't know how to ask about my grandfather. I wanted to know why he lived by himself in a run-down shack in some forgotten farming town with dirty tractor parts piled on the kitchen table and even dirtier dishes stacked in the sink, why he was happy my grandmother left him, why he drank so much and didn't take care of himself, and why he never came for Christmas or even mailed a birthday card. So many unknowns. Even as I grew older, I still felt like I couldn't ask these questions. I knew something was there, but I tiptoed around it. The obscurity that enveloped him always felt deliberately constructed, though I don't think he had any willing accomplices to help support his obfuscation. His story had become a taboo of sorts, not because it was a secret per se, but because it was unknown and because folks didn't talk about those sorts of things.

What really happened to my grandfather during the war? Something *must* have happened, we all thought. How bad was that tank battle, really? Did his tank survive? Or was he hit and had to save himself somehow? And what about that Japanese soldier he captured? Why were they patrolling on foot? What happened to the tanks? How did he treat the prisoners he came in contact after that day? Did he start to hate the treacherous bastards the same way his lieutenant had? What does it even mean to "mop up" after a battle is mostly over? Did he lose any friends? Did he ever kill anyone? No one could be sure. None of us knew the details of what he experienced, except for witnessing the mental and emotional damage these things left in their wake.

About seven years ago, I started asking questions again, looking for answers. I was tired of the silence and the secrets. The most tired I'd ever felt. I was tired of the guessing and the pretending, the lack of curiosity. The fake acceptance. The fear of acceptance. My father has avoided his memories like a man who makes peace with the scars from a car accident he can't bring himself to remember. It's in the past. Forget it. It doesn't matter now, anyway. But I can't. I'm not like my father. I can't pretend the past isn't real. I can't accept that we do not know the truth. I can't just walk away from the smoke and the muffled screams of the overturned car in the ditch that is my family's past. I can't ignore the blood splattered on the road. I have to search. I have to investigate. I have to make sense of it all.

DAVID CHRISINGER is the Director of Writing Seminars for *The War Horse*, the only non-profit newsroom that focuses specifically on issues related to the military and post-9/11 veterans. Chrisinger is also the editor of *See Me for Who I Am*, a collection of essays written by student veterans he taught at the University of Wisconsin-Stevens Point that aims to help bridge the cultural gap that divides his students form the American people they fought to protect. He lives in Wisconsin with his wife, Ashley, and their two young sons.

GINA HERRERA

Artist Statement

I have always felt a strong affinity for nature. Growing up in Chicago, I found the most beauty in the trees, the singing birds, the sky above. As a visual learner with a multicultural heritage, I have been influenced by my father's Tesuque culture and my mother's Costa Rican heritage. While cultural art fascinates me, experiencing beauty of great European art collections while stationed in Germany early in my military career inspired my professional pursuit of art.

While serving in Iraq, amid the devastation of combat, I was moved by seeing miles of mountainous trash heaps. I viscerally experienced the global extent of the systematic destruction of the planet, exploitative, unsustainable, and perhaps worst, careless, unconscious, accidental. This led me to question my own practices, hoping to lessen my environmental impact. I began to build three-dimensional forms out of discarded and natural objects. I am engaged in an aesthetic and spiritual ritual to channel and honor Mother Earth, to seek connection and communion with a power greater than myself.

Everywhere I go, I gather materials, finding inspiration in my surroundings. Like a scavenger, I play an interventional role in removing garbage from the landscape, preventing it from doing further damage. I am also drawn to natural materials and organic forms—branches, rocks, cocoons, nests. My process is meditative and intuitive—each step revealing a new aspect. Figures emerge, in gravity defying postures on the brink of movement, alive with possibility. Their haunting spiritual presence reminds us they have not gone back to the earth, but asks us to question our connection with our world and the choices we make in our daily existence. My greatest objective is to awaken individual and societal consciousness; to examine and heal our relationship with Mother Earth.

GINA HERRERA was raised in Chicago and currently resides in California. She has a BFA in Art Education from the School of the Art Institute of Chicago. In the course of her studies, she was deployed overseas in support of several war contingencies with the United States Army. Once her final tour was complete, she obtained her MFA from the University of the Arts in Philadelphia. Herrera is a multiple Art Slant Showcase Winner and has received grants from both the Chenven Foundation and Puffin Foundation. She has also received several awards and fellowships throughout the United States.

A Salutation to All

77" x 50" x 19"

Nurturing the Uncharted

78" x 44" x 31"

A Belle of Consequence

76" x 44" x 47"

Jaunting for Restitution

74" x 47" x 18"

Matrimony

65" x 25" x 18"

Rocking for the Future

85" x 54" x 21"

HANNAH DELA CRUZ ABRAMS

Songs for Ghosts

Northern Mariana Islands, 1992

Late at night we sing, my cousin Laurena and I, to drive the ghosts away. Earlier we made our own dinner, fried eggs and SPAM and rice with ketchup. Now, sitting up side by side on the concrete counter of the outdoor kitchen, we smoke our mothers' thin, menthol cigarettes. Our wrists delicate as eggshells. We let the blue plumes drift up from our mouths to our noses. We don't need anyone. I am twelve. She is fourteen. Our bodies are weightless. Young girls, bird-thin, singing to keep the ghosts away. *Amazing Grace. Silent Night. The Star-Spangled Banner.* We sing every song we know, drink wine coolers, dangle destroyed rubber zoris from our dry and dusty feet. A purple orchid startles out from the trunk of a tree. Long lines of bulbous red ants labor up the walls of the empty house. Laurena's shoulder is smooth against mine. Our hair is a single bramble under twin beaching crowns. A dog howls from the dense bamboo. We howl along with it. Somewhere in the dark and tangled woods, my mother stirs in a flimsy tent, throws a leg over her lover's hip, moves her face into the space between his shoulder blades. If there is a moon, Laurena and I don't see it. If the stars are kindled, we aren't looking. On the other end of the island, Laurena's mother slumps at a poker machine with our other five aunts. They slip in one dollar, five dollars, twenty dollars. They breathe softly and contentedly in the blue light. The whole world is worn out, drugged and sleeping. But we, Laurena and I, are wide awake, keeping vigil, raising our voices, throwing our arms around each other, and letting the high-pitched sound of our hoarse and drunken singing ring out into the night. We are singing away the ghosts, the specters and the spooks. Singing away the white lady who stuffs the souls of children into coconuts. The taotaomona tree spirits. And all our dead, loved ones who walk toward us wearing their favorite clothes. We sing and counter-sing. We could walk on any precipice and not fall, swim in the Trench and never drown. And yet, we are already winging away from each other, driven to fledge by the murmuration of cells in Laurena's belly. A top-speed division of us, of the world into Before and After. The division is a secret that will grow and grow until it splits her narrow body, leaves a narrow scar. Twenty years later, I will learn that the thing to fear is not behind you, that the hardest road can look like river, and that feathers are heavier than skeletons. Sitting up side by side on the concrete counter of the outdoor kitchen, we smoke our mothers' thin, menthol cigarettes, Laurena and I.

HANNAH DELA CRUZ ABRAMS was awarded the Whiting Writers Award for her novella *The Man Who Danced with Dolls* and her memoir-in-progress *The Following Sea.* She has also received a Rona Jaffe National Literary Award and a North Carolina Arts Council Fellowship. Her work has most recently appeared in the *Oxford American*, *StoryQuarterly*, *Mayday Magazine,* and *The Southern Humanities Review*, among others. Abrams currently teaches in the Department of English at the University of North Carolina Wilmington.

KOREY WILLIAMS

Mondays in Autumn

After Robert Hayden

Besides the whish of pleated skirts in time
with peeving birdsong; besides her mouthing
of old school hymns like Blessed Assurance;
and even besides her cue of Chanel No. 5,
its familiar question purpled in early light—

silent. Before heading downtown, hair curled and laid,
our mother would light on our bottom bunk,
control in hand, and we'd titter every time:
her tries at Dixie Kong's hair spin, practice for when

she drove out with a tennis racket that junky
who pissed and squatted in the yard. "I got three
little ones inside," she swore. "They can't see all of this,"
swatting on the edges of which we laid claim.
Now, tossed and wanting, I love you deliberately.

KOREY WILLIAMS grew up in suburban Chicago and studied at Illinois Wesleyan University, the University of Oxford, and Cornell University. He was a finalist in the 2017 National Poetry Series and his work appears in *Assaracus*, *Fogged Clarity*, *Winter Tangerine*, *The Offing*, *Narrative Magazine*, and elsewhere. Williams is currently a doctoral student at the University of Chicago.

CAITLIN MCGILL

Uncertainty

On a night when I'm sleeping beside David I dream I'm in his kitchen, washing dishes and counting calories in my head, peering out the window at the snow and feeling someone's presence beside me. I'm in *David's* apartment, washing *his* dishes, but when I look over my shoulder it's not David I see.

Carlos.

This is all wrong.

Suddenly I'm fully aware that I'm not with David, the man I met more than two years ago, a few months after leaving Carlos, leaving Florida. Instead I'm with Carlos again—or, as ever. *All wrong.* I gasp, my helium balloon lungs commandeering the space in my chest and I realize what will follow me into consciousness as fear—*How did I get stuck here again, how did he persuade me to let him back in?*

In the dream, the idea that I have been with Carlos for some time and have not, until this moment, been able to perceive that I should run is more startling than the image of Carlos hovering over my shoulder. More startling, perhaps, than the memory of his fist punching a perfect hole in the wall and then disappearing.

I wake and press my hand against my belly. Feel for fullness. Hope for emptiness. For proof that I am in control. I pull David's navy comforter to my chin, lace my naked foot into his, and watch gray clouds swallow the moon outside his third-floor window.

Some dreams wake you suddenly and frequently throughout the night, but others are subtler, quieter, harder to recall when you've woken yet impossible to forget. Frustrating, they are, because though you can't quite remember why they feel so absolutely important, they do, and because, though you can't determine if it's even wise to pursue them, to chase them down the trails of your memory, it seems you have no choice. Some dreams overpower you.

Lately, since I began speaking about Carlos in therapy, these sorts of dreams harass my waking life more than the ones that appear suddenly, vividly, coherently.

One week after the kitchen dream I lie beside David again, my head nestled against his shoulder, his arm resting on my lower back. Outside his window, beneath the streetlamp's glow, golden snowflakes flutter in the wind like fireflies. Again, I dream. This time the confusion, the panic, does not hit me so quickly. My life appears as it should, for the most part: In the dream I'm in Boston; I'm still a graduate student at Emerson College; I'm in a building I seem to recognize—at Emerson; I'm moving into an apartment that shows no signs of Carlos.

But, where is David?

In six months we're moving in together but here I am in this dream showing a friend my new apartment, an on-campus unit in this familiar structure—which makes this part of the dream inaccurate; this building is all classrooms and offices and library. Something's off. Here I am showing my friend that the apartment's so spacious it fits three, but since I'm completing my final semester of graduate school and since I teach here, too, I get the whole thing.

My living room is dark blue walls and dim lighting and emptiness. Red and yellow diamonds pattern the carpet floors. The bathroom's still missing everything—toilet paper, toothpaste, even a toothbrush. It seems it's morning and I haven't even brushed my teeth yet.

Perhaps reality is sneaking its way into my sleep.

In another room: a glass, floor-to-ceiling wall. Beyond that: what appears to be an aquarium. This is my living space. *How wonderful*, I think, but don't truly feel it because: Where is David? Where are those blue eyes and those nail-bitten fingers pointing to his favorite buildings and the growing moon?

I take my friend back into the barren living room and run my hands along the carpet floor.

"All this space," I say, excited at the thought of spreading two hundred pages of my writing around the room and shuffling, finding order.

When we leave we are on a bus and a new girl stands beside me. She is a silhouette. No discernible face. I tell her it's okay that she doesn't know who she is, but not to go around wasting time without a passion, a drive, an idea of what she's living for, and then David is beside me, holding on as the bus barrels down an expressway, sunlight streaming in. There is David telling this aimless girl she needs a plan, needs to get it together, giving her a hard time really. It's not like him, the architect who almost always smiles. I tell her *it's okay*.

And then David and the bus are gone.

The girl—let's call her Cate—and I are walking backward on the side of that expressway, grass brushing our ankles, cars speeding toward our backs though we can't see them until they pass. I haven't seen green grass and sunny skies like this in so long that I'm not so bothered by those approaching cars or the enigmatic reason we are walking backwards. I should be.

The grassy hill beside us slopes toward a canal and there is Carlos, this time in a small car that he lets roll toward the water. I'm certain the car is going to sink and be lost for good, but when its nose grazes the surface, it stops. Carlos and a small chestnut dog emerge from the vehicle. The dog starts to pee and I start to scold Carlos and then the dog stops and I tell her no, no, go ahead, you need to go, and she runs off and there we are, wading in the green grass beneath sunny skies, and I am wondering, somewhere between sleep and awake, *Is this what would have been? Me in a graduate apartment in another school, perhaps not Emerson after all, chasing him and our sweet dog down expressways, who I was or who I might have been a shadow chasing him—chasing me?*

I am relieved that in this scene Carlos is not yelling or crying or violent. Still: he is there. Cate is gone.

I wake and wrap my arms around David, trace my fingers across his broad back until he pulls me closer. I look to the window across the room and watch snow dance around in the real world outside. I try to forget about green grass and sunny skies.

During my weekly meeting with my psychologist, the one who's helping me realize that Carlos might still be hidden inside me, that trauma is trying to claw its way out, that my powerlessness to fully recall and understand our history might be complicit in my need for control—might've awakened my eating disorder—I tell her about the dream I had last week.

"I was standing in the kitchen," I say, "washing dishes, but Carlos was in David's place and the scene was all wrong."

Finally she asks, "Do you think there's anything to that—that he was in the *kitchen* with you?"

That night I dream of Emerson students jumping from the seventh floor of residential buildings. They're jumping because apparently that's a *thing* right now—jumping into piles of snow that, during this record-breaking winter, stand three and four feet high on Boston's sidewalks. In the dream they jump and I urge them not to, and my family is there, and my friends are there, and the only person who seems to think this absurd is me. And then I'm sitting on the sidewalk with my head in my hands, angry and frustrated and unsure how to stop this insanity, and there is Carlos—again—and I'm more angry and frustrated than I was moments earlier because I'm certain, very certain, that I never wanted him here. That is clear.

I wake up and know what happened and know I don't want him beside my body, in a dream or in waking life. I write it down. Seal it shut. Begin my day. Try not to count calories.

But then another dream arrives two nights after I meet with my psychologist, a dream in which I am telling Carlos, *Look, I cannot be with you anymore; I have been miserable for months—years—and I do not want to stay.* I am, temporarily, sure of my words. I am shaking with the need to say this, with the fleeting certainty of my belief. So, what's unclear?

Soon Carlos is crying and convincing me, somehow, that this isn't exactly true—that my feelings, my desires, are actually *not correct.* I'm listening to him persuade me against what I believed were my own deep beliefs, persuade me that maybe my feelings *are* truly wrong, that maybe I've forgotten the magic behind *us* that means we should be together, want to be together, *must* be together. That I should hold on just a little longer, even when his knuckles bruise my car fenders and steering wheel. Suddenly I am acquiescing to his words, looking down at my toes and running a hand through my hair; suddenly my beliefs are no longer mine, at least I don't think they are though I'm not quite sure anymore, and I have lost all control of my own true desires and am beginning to think he's right, that I do want him after all.

I don't leave.

When I wake I begin to wonder if therapy—speaking of Carlos aloud, willingly recalling those memories instead of repressing them or waiting for them to harass me—might be healing my body but further assaulting my mind. My brain a set of long dormant volcanoes suddenly poked and prodded and shaken to life. Carlos erupting from them in my dreams.

The next day I'm irritable, withdrawn, unable to free my mind of him in my waking life, and though I've tried to take him out of dreams and write him into words, I still can't shake the fright that's quivering inside my skull. How has he made me question my decision to leave him in waking life, if he's only speaking to me in dreams? What more can I do to erase him from me?

That night as I roll side to side and envy David's soundless sleep, as his tangible body grazes my belly, I begin to count what I can actually see. There's the window. *One.* And there's the streetlamp, the snowy fireflies. *Two, three.* No clouds tonight. A single star punctures the sky's curtain, the moon slashing the black sheet. *Three four five.*

David inhales.

Silence.

And then finally he exhales, air gliding out of that palpable body like water streaming down a creek. *I might not sleep tonight,* I think, *but at least I will not dream.*

CAITLIN MCGILL is a 2016 St. Botolph Emerging Artist Award winner and Bread Loaf Writers' conference scholarship recipient. She was also the 2014 winner of the Rafael Torch Nonfiction Literary Award. Her work has appeared or is forthcoming in Blackbird, Consequence, Crab Orchard Review, Gravel, Iron Horse Literary Review, Vox, and several other magazines. Currently, she is working on a memoir about her family's hidden past, intergenerational trauma, inherited survival mechanisms, immigration, race, class, addiction, and the cost of ignoring our histories. One essay from her book was named a Notable Essay in The Best American Essays 2016.

TERESA FAZIO

Ridgeline

First of the month means a paycheck, and Friday morning means a long run. So there's a bounce in my step as I walk to the squat brick warehouse for our eight-Marine section. Lance Corporal Dino's outside, sucking the last of his predawn cigarette. He grinds the cherry out under his sneaker and flicks it my way. The white blip arcs overhead.

"I'm not the one who's gonna be picking up trash this weekend," I say. His jaw tightens. He retrieves the butt and drops it into the sand-filled coffee can by the door.

"You're in charge, *Corporal* Hugo," he spits. He's still pissed about my promotion—two hundred bucks extra each month—but I'm not the one who told him to get a DUI last year.

I *am* the one, though, who wrote his name on the duty roster for Saturday morning, which I admit was kind of shitty.

The ma'am comes out in those silky green uniform shorts that no one looks good in. Friday mornings she runs us in the ridgeline— the hilly trails behind our building. The rest of the shop files out, circles up. The ma'am stands on one leg and pulls the opposite ankle; her pale quad shines. Dino cracks his knuckles when we lean down to stretch our hamstrings. We start the run easy enough. Sun breaks over yellowed scrub. Dew soaks our sneakers. Then the ma'am turns uphill.

"Blood makes the grass grow, kill kill kill!" Dino shouts with feigned motivation.

We should have been friends. We were both in the same class at electronics repair school. We competed to see who could make the most perfect fiber splice, who could puzzle out circuit problems faster. We stood in parallel lines at the Navy Fed, carving fifties from our biweekly checks to send back to our respective Mamís. We hit the fleet at the same time, in the same unit. He'd once been our fastest runner, but as he smoked more and I trained harder, we evened up. He was always a dick, but didn't seem to hold it against me that I was female. Not until after his DUI. Last month, when I was promoted meritoriously and he was not, I could sense his frown in formation, his lips pressed together too hard.

The terrain turns gnarly; we huff and curse in low voices. The ma'am takes us up Radio Hill, towards the tower that blinks red atop it. It's the steepest run we know; everyone hates it except our masochist lieutenant. My foot slips on scree, and I nearly lose my balance. Pebbles tumble behind me. Dino snickers, and though we all slow down, I begin imperceptibly to fall behind.

The ma'am is twenty yards ahead; her brown bob sways in rhythm with her steps. She must do this for fun on weekends. Maybe she grew up in the Rockies. Or maybe they supply drugs at Officer Candidates School. Creatine. Erythropoetin. My lungs scream.

"C'mon Hugo, where you at?" Dino says behind me, all quiet-psycho. "You slowin' down?

"Shut it, Dino," I say, irritated.

"Ohhh, are we cranky? We on the rag this week, *Corporal*?" he says just loud enough so I can hear. The ma'am seems not to notice.

"Fuck off," I say, and pump my legs. This hill is murder.

I hear Dino closing in. He pulls up alongside me, although the trail is narrow. Soon we're in a full-on race to the top. He edges me out, kicking up small chunks of gravel. He says nothing, hands atop his head, broad joker mouth grinning. Motherfucker.

I stumble the last few steps up the hill, put my hands behind my head, tip my chin to the sky. The other Marines follow, strung out over a full minute's run of scrub.

"Attaway, Corporal Hugo," the ma'am says.

Dino looks me in the eye with his sarcastic smile. "Just a little run uphill, ain't it, *Corporal*?" he says, breathing evenly.

"Fuckin' a, *Lance* Corporal," I say between gasps. And then, louder—"I'd order you to drive me back to the office, but I'm not sure you've got your car keys back."

His eyes go slack, like a little boy's. The hurt on his face makes even me wince. He looks at the ground, takes a breath. Then steps closer. "Got 'em back last week, you—"

"Let's go," barks the ma'am. She waves a hand at Dino. "Speedy Gonzales, get in front here and lead us home."

I admit it was a dick thing to say, but he had it coming.

That afternoon, the safety brief is the usual don't-drink-and-drive-use-condoms. All of us can repeat the ma'am's phrases word for word. You'd think we'd listen, but if we did, Dino would be a Corporal, and my roommate Maria wouldn't have that stretch of months after her deployment she doesn't talk about.

My roommates Maria and Benson work in admin. Most days Benson wears her blond hair in a French braid, but come Friday afternoon, she's in front of the mirror, wielding a blow-dryer and slathering crap on her face. Maria calls me by my last name since we have the same first name. Sunday mornings, she comes home with stories. Meeting Jay-Z in an LA club. Hitching back to base when her car broke down at Coachella. We're like the cast of *Girls* mashed with *Generation Kill*, and you can guess which ones like to party.

Every weekend my roommates try a new tactic to pry me from the barracks and get me hammered, so all summer I studied for the Corporal's boards. I faked a headache two weeks ago and cramps last week.

I don't like bars, especially not with other Marines around. How can you face troops Monday morning if they know how you look sloppy-drunk? Running—that I can do. Flailing on a dance floor? Nuh-uh. Besides, guys don't hit on me, in my jeans and scuffed sandals. And if they did? In front of everyone? Word would get back to jackasses like Dino. So most Fridays, I hit the laundry, gym, maybe a movie. It's lonely, but it's easier. And I guess it's worth it to get ahead. I mean—I picked up meritorious Corporal, didn't I?

But when I return to our room after the safety brief, I see the one dress from my wall locker laid out on my bed. "C'mon, you're an NCO now," Maria says, olive skin glowing, her dark hair curling around the iron. "You can have a little fun. You haven't even had a promotion party."

I'm tired from the morning's run, and still pissed at Dino. Fuck it. Just one drink.

"Fine," I say. "I need a beer. Clowns in my section get on my nerves."

"Yeah!" she says. "Sushi Samba?"

"Whatever."

Benson barges in, holding a no-shit grocery bag full of makeup. "Trick or treat!" she says, holding it out.

"I think that works the other way around," I say.

I let her flutter a mascara wand across my lashes. She lends me vanilla lip balm, which I know I'll scrape off with my teeth by the time we get to the car. It takes me two minutes to slide on my dress and Rainbow flip-flops. But tubes and crimpers occupy Maria and Benson the rest of the hour.

Their cackling sounds like the delinquent girls in my Catholic high school, primping and smoking at cracked porcelain sinks. Meanwhile, I scurried to class, mindful of wasting Mamí's hard-earned dollars. The nuns clucked *make something of yourselves*, and we all did—within a year, those girls made babies. I made it through boot camp.

I'm resigned to reading *Us Weekly* when something soft and black lands in my lap.

"Put that on," Maria says.

"It's like half a sweater."

"It's called a bolero. It goes with your dress."

"Is this even clothing? It doesn't have pockets."

"Just put it on."

A tiny purse sails by my head. It's too small to fit my phone, but I take it anyway, drop my Samsung into my desk drawer for safekeeping.

By the time we leave, it's drizzling. I duck into the backseat of Maria's Jetta, slouched and self-conscious. As the car glides off base, I feel nervous. They do this every weekend, but I can't remember the last time I went out.

Parking's a bitch in downtown Oceanside. We find a lot a quarter-mile from the beachside sushi joint. The girls clip-clop in their heels, and my sandals flap. Sand and grit film my toes. The bar's packed; Benson marshals us through. Silver eye shadow rims her lids, and her tan legs are muscled beneath her short skirt. We order small plates of things we can eat standing up: California rolls and skewered teriyaki. It's too loud to talk.

The bartender's in a tight black t-shirt, like Simon Cowell. He hands me a canned Sapporo. Maria and Benson get frozen margaritas. They take dainty sips, scan the dance floor, shoot each other looks over my head. I stand awkwardly, gulping my beer. Maria angles her head to point out a hottie. Benson laughs.

"We're gonna go to the bathroom," they say. "You all right?" They've tried to include me—they really have—but they have rounds to make, a dance floor to prowl, boys to capture. They slip twenties under my plate and disappear.

I turn towards the bar, nurse my beer. I would play with my phone, but it's back in my desk drawer. The bartender pities me, pours a tequila and winks. "On me," he says. I down it and order a margarita, pushing aside my half-full beer. Maybe I can take small dainty sips.

When the bartender hands me the cup, I feel a shove from behind. Half my margarita sloshes out. An elbow swings away. Someone kicks my bare heel. I grimace and grab the bar, letting the pain subside.

"Watch the lady," a voice says from above, then asks, "You okay? Mind if I slide in?" I turn to a crisp white shirt over broad shoulders, shiny black hair. His half-sleeve tattoo is all red flowers, like a Hawaiian shirt. "Nice ink," I say into almond eyes.

"Thanks," he says, "grew up on the big island." I think, *well, aloha*, but you can't say that out loud without sounding like a tool.

I screw up my courage fast. "Can I buy you a drink?" I ask. He looks at me quizzically, bends closer, motions to his ear. He hasn't heard me. I stand on tiptoe. "Can I buy you a drink?"

He gives me a bemused smile. "Sorry, I'm on a beer run myself," he says. He jerks his head back. "Girlfriend and all."

I look down at the bar. *Of course. I'm supposed to stand here and bat my eyelashes. I suck at this.* I add my twenty to the pile under my plate and turn to go.

"For a short chick, you're cute, though," he says as I step away. Nice of him. Still, doesn't help.

Someone taps my back, and I jump. It's a middle-aged lady, weaving a little, her lipstick smeared. Brownish roots peek from under her streaks of blond. "Honey, your tag's out," she says. She flips the bolero's size tag back in, pats my back again.

I push through the crowd. This—*this*—is why I never go out. I glimpse Maria and Benson on the tiny dance floor. They sandwich some guy with an open shirt; he holds a Corona aloft. I cross the room to a sliding door; it opens to a low wooden deck, a few stairs to the beach. I shut the door behind me, the raucous bar silenced.

It's cold out, but dry. The clouds have cleared; stars glitter over the water. I pull the bolero tight to my chest, fasten its one button. A shrimp tail's stuck to the bottom of my sandal. I sit down on the top stair, take off my shoe, and scrape it against the deck. The ocean belches rubbery kelp onto the sand.

A couple walks across my field of view, silhouetted against the ocean, holding hands. Loneliness wells up and washes over me. Meritorious Corporal doesn't mean much now. My throat closes, and my eyes spill over. I peel the damp cocktail napkin from my cup and press it to my eyelids. It does nothing to stanch the tears. One, two ugly sobs. I hate myself for crying.

I don't know how long I sit with my face in my hands before I hear the commotion. The sliding door shrieks behind me. Men yell curses. Sounds like three against one. If I curl my head down further, maybe they won't notice me. "No, fuck *you*," one says. Still, I don't look. Then a sting on my back, thud-thud *whap* as one of them trips over me and falls down two short steps, off the deck. He grunts as he lands in the sand. Laughter from the three hulking voices. They leave the door open; out tumble rap beats and loud conversations.

Sweat plasters my bangs to my forehead. I raise my eyes to squint at the fallen man. He's on his back, struggling to sit up. High-and-tight haircut, cargo shorts, gold chain. His nose trickles blood.

"You all right?" I ask, though I don't really care. He pinches the bridge of his nose. Then he blinks and stares straight at me, gives me a weird smile.

Spooked, I get up with a quickness. The tiny purse flaps at my side as I turn away. I follow laughter across the bar. It sounds like Benson's, high and screechy. But in the corner from which it came, I can find neither her nor Maria. I should text them, but—no phone. I circle the bar once, twice. Check the bathroom—no sign. Maybe they're outside. They're not.

I retrace our steps to where I think Maria parked her car. The lot's near-empty. I see no Jettas, just a dressed-up couple making out in an SUV. The last thing I want to do is knock on their window to borrow a phone. At the edge of the lot, I claim a pool of light and wonder if cabs ever drive down this street. Expensive, even if they do.

A white Honda Del Sol cruises towards me, bass so loud it buzzes. The front bumper glows unpainted yellow. A rosary swings from the rearview. Marine Corps stickers. The driver slows to a crawl, rolls down his window, angles his head. I step forward, ashamed but relieved, and— this is stupid— tears well again. Through their blur, I could almost mistake the guy for Dino.

I open my mouth to ask for a ride, but before I can get out a word, he shifts to a higher gear and speeds away.

A cigarette butt flies out the car window. Orange sparks strike the pavement. I take a few steps in my flip-flops and choke down the lump in my throat.

I look up, wipe my raccoon eyes, and try to gauge the distance to base. It seems impossibly far, where the red dot on the radio tower blinks over the ridgeline.

TERESA FAZIO was a Marine Corps communications officer from 2002-2006, deploying once to Iraq. Her writing has been published in the *New York Times*, *Rolling Stone*, *Task and Purpose*, and *Penthouse*, among other outlets. She has contributed to the anthologies *The Road Ahead*, *Retire the Colors*, and *It's My Country, Too.* Her memoir manuscript *Unbecoming* was a finalist in nonfiction contests from Autumn House Press and Dzanc Books. She lives, works, and writes in New York City.

NATALIE LOVEJOY

Artist Statement

In 2008, I was an Army wife, writer, and composer stationed at Ft. Campbell, KY. My then-husband was a soldier deployed to Iraq for a year. I noticed the military world I was experiencing was rarely accurately represented in entertainment, much less musical theater. This world was one composed of complex, apolitical, and full of real individuals struggling to find meaning in their lives like everyone else. As someone from a completely civilian background, this experience forever changed me, and I found myself determined to write a musical that would allow civilians to have a similar experience. In addition, I wanted service members to see themselves authentically represented in a piece of musical theater. As a result, I started writing *Deployed.*

The following song, "Battle Scars" is part of a subplot between a Specialist and an MP during the deployment in Iraq. Though they both have developed feelings for each other, they are blocked by their own assumed prejudices: She feels resentment over the suspicion that he doesn't take her seriously as a soldier, and he holds back out of the fear that she has stereotyped him as just a dumb "grunt." In this scene and song, they finally find some common ground.

An excerpt from *Deployed*

ACT ONE

SCENE 6

The barracks, a few days later. Lights up on the soldiers watching a movie. They lean forward, very serious and intently absorbed. We hear the romantic, emotional score of Beauty and the Beast, *and then the Beast says, "You came back." SOLDIER 1 sniffles loudly.*

SPECIALIST

Are you fucking *crying?*

SOLDIER 3

Shhh!

(They continue to watch, completely engrossed. The SPECIALIST gets up and turns it off. Everyone boos at him.)

SOLDIER 2

That's the best part of the whole movie!

SPECIALIST

It's a fucking cartoon, you pussies.

(He leaves the tent in a huff and sits on a bench outside, smoking. Lights out on the other soldiers. The MP enters and walks over to the SPECIALIST.)

MP

Something came for you.

SPECIALIST

Really? (He takes the package and looks at the wrapping.) Is this M.R.E. paper?

MP

Just fucking open it!

(He unwraps it. It's a package of cigarettes.)

Oh, cool. These are my favorite. (He reads the attached card.) "Merry Christmas. Lung cancer kills." (He smiles.) Thank you.

MP

So what's going on with your folks?

SPECIALIST

I've just been on so many deployments sending care packages isn't fun for them anymore, I guess. What about yours?

MP

Um, yeah, same. (Beat) So where's my gift, asshole?

[MUSIC IN: NO. 12 "BATTLE SCARS"]

SPECIALIST

I'll stop giving you a hard time…for today.

MP

You know, grunts are the only ones doing shit out here.

SPECIALIST

Yeah, but we're the ones getting all fucked up. (He lifts up his shirt, revealing a large scar on his side.) See this? That was from a huge-ass piece of shrapnel I took during a patrol once. They had to remove a rib. (She rolls her eyes at him.) I have one less rib than you!

MP

So?
I HAVE A SCAR HERE ON MY SHOULDER —

SPECIALIST

I GOT A SCAR THERE, TOO.

MP

A BULLET BARELY MISSED -

SPECIALIST

MORE SHRAPNEL.

MP

THAT SHIT JUST DOESN'T LIKE YOU.

SPECIALIST

HERE'S ANOTHER ON MY FOREHEAD
FROM A BLAST -

MP

YEP, SAME HERE.
(Showing him the scar under her hair)
LOOK YOU CAN SEE IT.

SPECIALIST

MINE IS WORSE.

MP

OH?

SPECIALIST

IT KNOCKED MY BRAINS OUT.

MP

YEAH, THAT'S CLEAR...

SPECIALIST

I NEEDED A STITCH!

MP

AND I WAS SEEING STARS!

SPECIALIST

Whatever...

MP

YOU'RE NOT THE ONLY ONE WITH BATTLE SCARS.

(The SPECIALIST tosses his cigarette.)

SPECIALIST

Ok, time for the big guns. (Gesturing to his arm muscles) Get it?

MP

Oh, you're funny, too.

SPECIALIST

I MIGHT AS WELL SHOW YOU THIS ONE.

MP

IS THAT A HEART?

SPECIALIST

YEAH, IT WAS.

MP

AND SOMEONE'S NAME?

SPECIALIST

RELAX, IT'S ALMOST GONE NOW.

MP

I BET THAT HURTS.

SPECIALIST

YES, IT DOES...

(The MP pulls back her shirt, revealing a tattoo of a man's name.)

MP

I'VE GOT SOME INK AS WELL HERE.

SPECIALIST

(Threatened)

WHO IS THAT?

MP

JUST A GUY I KNEW.
HE WAS KILLED ON OUR LAST DEPLOYMENT.

SPECIALIST

YEAH, I KNEW A FEW OF THOSE, TOO...

BOTH

NOT EVERYONE WOULD LIVE THROUGH SCRAPES LIKE OURS.
YOU'RE NOT THE ONLY ONE WITH BATTLE SCARS.

SPECIALIST

I'M BROKEN AND BATTERED,

MP

I'M CUT UP AND SHATTERED,

SPECIALIST

I'VE GOT SCARS YOU CAN'T SEE.

MP
IT'S THE SAME WAY WITH ME.

SPECIALIST
I'M SCARED THAT THEY'LL SCARE YOU.

MP
I'M SCARED YOU'LL BE SCARED, TOO.

SPECIALIST	MP
THEY NEVER GO AWAY,	
	THEY NEVER GO AWAY,
BUT EVERY SINGLE SCAR	
	BUT EVERY SINGLE SCAR
MAKES YOU WHO YOU ARE	

BOTH
AND I LIKE WHO YOU ARE TODAY.

I'VE BEEN BURNED AND DRAGGED
THROUGH EVERY KIND OF WAR,

SPECIALIST
BUT I'M NOT THE ONLY ONE,

MP
I'M NOT THE ONLY ONE,

SPECIALIST
I'M NOT THE ONLY ONE,

MP
I'M NOT THE ONLY ONE -

SPECIALIST

I'M NOT THE ONLY ONE -

BOTH

ANYMORE.

(The SPECIALIST leans forward to kiss her, and his hand is immediately clipped by a mousetrap that the M.P planted earlier.)

SPECIALIST

Mother-fucker!!

(They laugh. Music and lights out.)

Battle Scars

from *Deployed*

Music and Lyrics by
Natalie Lovejoy

12

MP: A bul - let bare - ly missed... That shit just does - n't like__ you.

SPC: More shrap - nel.

14

MP: Yep, same here.

SPC: Here's a - no - ther on my fore - head... from a blast.

16

MP: Look, you can see it. Oh? Yeah, that's clear... And

SPC: Mine is worse. It knocked my brains out! I need-ed a stitch!

MP
I was see - ing stars!
You're not the on - ly one with bat - tle scars.
M.P.
Is that a heart?
SPC
I might as well show you this one.
Yeah, it was.
mp
And some'one name..
I bet that hurts.
I've got some ink as well here.
Re - lax, it's al - most gone now.
Yes, it does...

30
MP
Just a guy I knew. He was killed on our last de-ploy-ment. Not
SPC
Who is that?? Yeah... I knew a few of those, too...
30
33
MP
ev - 'ry-one would live through scrapes like ours. You're not the on - ly one
SPC
Not ev-'ry-one would live through scrapes like ours. You're not the on - ly one
33
37
MP
with bat-tle scars. I'm
SPC
with bat-tle scars. I'm brok-en and bat - tered.
37
mp

41
MP
cut up and shat - tered. It's the same way with me.
SPC
I've got scars you can't see. I'm
44
MP
I'm scared you'll be scared, too. They ne ver go a - way, but ev-'ry sin-gle
SPC
scared that they'll scare you. They ne-ver go a - way, but ev-'ry sin-gle scar
mf
mp
48
MP
scar makes you who you are, and I like who you are to - day.
SPC
makes you who you are, and I like who you are to - day.
pp

52

MP: I've been burned and dragged through ev - 'ry kind of war,

SPC: I've been burned and dragged through ev - 'ry kind of war,

mf

57

MP: I'm not the on - ly one,

SPC: but I'm not the on - ly one, I'm not the on - ly one,

f

61

MP: I'm not the on - ly one an - y - more.

SPC: I'm not the on - ly one an - y - more.

pp *rit.*

WHITNEY TERRELL

excerpt from *The Crossroads*

Systems had always been of interest to the Bonta men. Herman Bonta fought bravely in World War I, even though he knew Congress had declared Puerto Ricans to be U.S. citizens just so they could draft men like him. His grandson Ramon attended Pontifical Catholic in Ponce, settled into a mid-level insurance position with MetLife and, spurred by Herman's grit, got a transfer to Kansas City in 1986 where he sold policies in the Spanish-speaking Guadalupe and Argentine districts. Surfaces mattered, he taught his son, Ernesto. Appearances mattered. The system was designed to protect the group and the more you looked like the group, the mean, the better the system protected you. But his coffee table Picasso books and his fly rod and his hand-sewn gloves were sold after he died of a heart attack, when Ernesto was eight, because Ramon Bonta, it turned out, had skimped on his own protection. His life policy only paid $50,000. And their house, which had been purchased with a white real estate agent, in a white neighborhood, had to be sold at cost because the neighborhood was, thanks to suburban flight, already on its way out.

Ernesto continued to address himself to the system: thin, lithe, muscled, in white polos, and skinny jeans tucked into impeccable Nikes. A prow of gelled black hair. Not perfect. He knew that. Moles.

A twisted canine. Eyes slightly too close together. At rest, he had an air of stunned and watchful suspicion, as if someone had hit him, but he wasn't sure where. He was sure that premiums were lower across the board—life, health, car, and home—if you lived in a good neighborhood rather than a bad one. And that by the time he entered eighth grade, his family was renting in the same Mexican-American community his father had avoided *except* when selling policies. His mother waitressed for a white-owned taco restaurant with sombreros tacked to the wall. Ernesto shelved books at Barnes & Noble. He studied French. He got a scholarship and played soccer at Redemptorist High. He was good. But not good enough to pay for college. One spring afternoon during his senior year, he sat out on the un-swept back deck of his mother's house, and sorted through the musty remains of his father's files, watching the Gomez brothers slap plastic light sabers on the muddy slope of their back yard. A terrifying darkness awaited him and his sister, Diana. The files laid this out. Actuarial Charts. Morbidity Tables. Annual Income. Liabilities. At the very bottom of every chart were the poor, frozen in the deepest, coldest risk pool. But the charts were not always final. Sometimes, his father had told him, the best of his clients would manage to escape by briefly maxing out their risk, in the hope that such a gamble would slingshot them higher in the end. He scrounged through the bottom of the file box and, eyes on the Gomez brothers, lifted his great-grandfather's revolver onto his knees.

And so he joined the Army, bought a new Dodge Charger with his signing bonus (or made the down payment, anyway), completed basic training, and shipped out to Joint Base Balad as an operations specialist, prepping to take the sergeant's exam, in the winter of '08. He worked in his battalion's air-conditioned tactical operations center, on the fourth floor of a yellow brick building that reminded him of a public school back in the States. Linoleum floors, water fountains, dented metal elevators with those fat black buttons you saw in buildings from the 1960s. They sat in rows at plywood tables, fitted out with Panasonic Toughbooks. Beside him was Sergeant Keifer Morgan, his partner, his guide, though they rarely deployed any farther than their ten-foot square of desk space.

Between them, a folder marked SECRET that contained their current target's headshot, height, weight, eye color, aliases, and relatives, gathered in a page or two report called a Baseball Card, plus any other intel they had on the guy. Also research reports from Credit Suisse on the stocks that he and Morgan would be trading on that day. "Let's do a pairs trade," Morgan would say at nightfall, when they sat down to work. "Short Hassan Al-Khalid, this little shithead mukhtar, and long Wells Fargo into earnings. Booyah, mutherfuckers!"

Sergeant Morgan was black-haired and schlubby, not athletic, as Ernesto had been. His froggy eyes were so far apart that you could punch his nose and miss both. Which happened. Ernesto learned to pick him in the intra-company softball game so he didn't end up on the bench. Choose him as his secret Santa, so he didn't end up without a gift, and above all council him on women—especially Sergeant Lucy White, who worked in their maintenance platoon. But late at night in the TOC, when their commanding officer, Major Pickering—otherwise known as the S3—was away, Morgan was a master, brooked no fools, felt no regrets. They coordinated "current operations"—meaning they kept in contact with infantry on the ground, facilitated air support, helped pilots and the ground pounders identify their targets, and "clarified" whatever the rules of engagement were that week. Busy times. That year, they worked one hundred and eighty missions, which led to seventy arrests, thirty KIA. After each, they cleaned the desk of their target's artifacts and burned them according to protocol. Burn bags of Baseball Cards, an All Star roster of the naked and the dead. It was what he'd wanted, wasn't it? He was in the safest part of the system, glimpsing all the most precious information. No value was intrinsic. Morgan taught him that. A good trader was never wedded to a cause, to a belief, to a stock, even to a person. Truths Ernesto's father had missed. "These guys in the insurgency look like fucking idiots now," Morgan explained one night, while waiting to support a raid. "But they're just in a bear market. Experiencing consolidation. Five years from now, one of these same dudes will have survived. We'll have wiped out his competition and we'll be *selling* him weapons instead."

It was their commitment to this truth, heartless truth, that bound them together and kept them safe. And kept their families safe, since Ernesto was wiring more than half his salary home to his mother and sister, to pay for food, rent, and Diana's college tuition.

After a year, Morgan and Ernesto returned to Fort Hood with private sector prospects and good skills. They had blood on their hands, too, but that was added value, wasn't it? How many new employees at Palantir or Barracuda Networks could say they'd killed a man anywhere outside of a Play Station screen? Morgan had three months left on his Army contract; Ernesto had two years. But that did not stop him from taking a dry run on his own future along with Morgan, checking San Francisco real estate on Zillow, discussing stock options, checking the route lines of the Google bus, or the sushi selection at the Facebook cafeteria. That was the slingshot he'd imagined, where he moved past all those kids back at high school, when he accomplished something that even his father never dreamed, until an MP knocked on his apartment door outside Fort Hood and led him to CID, where he'd never been, and sat him in a conference room, with a camera up in the ceiling corner, so he'd know he was being seen. For an hour he sat there, then two. He did not ask questions; he did not cry out. He knew how this went. But that did not prevent him, in those two short silent hours, from wishing, with unspeakable terror and loathing, that he could cut his losses and disinvest himself from himself, because that's what everybody else would do to him, now that the cameras were turned his way.

So he didn't really examine the charges or ask for a JAG lawyer when the CID investigators came in with their dossiers, their logs of his emails, the lists of his computer searches he'd executed while supposedly working—highlighting the visits he'd made to his brokerage account at TD Ameritrade. Not even the typed up deposition from Sergeant Morgan. But he did watch the video from a Warthog's targeting system that had that morning leaked to the public, replicating itself on the internet and cable news. It included the recorded conversation between the pilot—

I don't know if this target is right.

—and a second voice, which was his:

Doesn't matter if it's right. Rules of Engagement say you can shoot. Just make it effective.

There's people moving around the building. I can't identify if they're armed or not. They may be noncombatants.

Bravo will make it look good when they go in, Eagle 2. Just give me my dead rag heads. My S3 isn't here and by the time I find him, it'll be too late. Finish it off. I am way too long Apple and the market's closing in New York, so I need to make a trade.

The S3, Major Pickering, really hadn't been there. But Morgan had been, slouched in the dark beside him, telling him what to say. They had always talked this way, Morgan especially. But the voice was his and once he saw the first line of Morgan's deposition—*That guy was a mad man. Reckless. The S3 and I had stepped outside just for a minute when this happened, or we would've stopped it immediately*—he knew he was on the short end of the trade.

His discharge was classified as Other Than Honorable. Silicon Valley was out. So, too, most contracting. No GI bill, no benefits. In one stroke of a pen, the entire reason he'd had for joining the Army was stripped away. He was marked, a broken stock, a washout—as Morgan had told him, a stock could keep going down for much longer than you'd ever think. Four years later, he moved back home to his mother's house at 18th and Summit, in the old Guadalupe Parish he'd originally hoped to escape. Like his sister, the neighborhood had moved on without him. A French patisserie had opened two blocks down, where Mr. Gomez's bodega had once been. A rap recording studio next door, a shop that sold hipster memorabilia, if such a thing was even sane. And on his own block, close enough that he could hear the noise and chatter at night, a restaurant and bar called West Side Pride, with bare brick walls and $15 glasses of Chardonnay and picnic tables in a side patio area that were hung with gaudy electric lights, like some white person's fantasy of what a Mexican bar might look like, filled with the kind of people who would've fit in perfectly well in . . . well, Silicon Valley. Did he get the irony? Copy that.

Mornings, he went to Reggie's Snack Bar, a hipster joint just down the hill from their house, and a place Ernesto had begun to frequent because it was cheap. His sister, perfumed, in a slinky taupe dress and massive heels, sat across from him. She ran social media for the Mayor and kept her phone face up while she stroked the back of his hand. "Ernesto—"

"Flea," he corrected. He'd adopted the name in California; someone on his roofing crew gave it to him because he rode on everybody else's back.

"—I just want to help you get better. You helped me, when I was little. And you paid for school. I believe in you. I did. I do—but you got to meet with somebody."

Everything I've ever taught you was wrong. That was the message that would help his sister. But when he tried to speak this warning, everything fell apart and *he* sounded like he was insane. "Yes," he said. "It's okay. Don't worry about it. I'll get some counseling. There's time to talk about these other things. Just maybe, I don't know, promise me one thing: promise you'll stay on the same side of the camera as me?"

His smile must have been horrifying, judging from how still she kept her face.

Diana went to work. The Flea sat there drinking coffee. That was when he met the owner, Reggie Burton. He was there in his café frequently: an unruly, hairy, burly man who wore an American flag bandanna around his head in the way old rockers did to cover up their thinning hair. Some days he sported a rumpled corduroy suit, wool time and cowboy boots; sometimes a wife beater and a track suit. An undercover person, with different uniforms for different days, none of them strictly true—which pretty much matched the style of the café.

"You're not wrong to worry about what side your sister's on, man," Burton was saying to him, some time later—time that The Flea hadn't really paid strict attention to passing. "If you've seen the bad side, you know what it looks like. But trying to explain that to someone who hasn't been there, that's a complicated thing. Try this book. They won't have it at the VA."

The colonialist makes history and he knows it, he read back at home. *And because he refers constantly to the history of this metropolis, he plainly indicates that here he is the extension of this metropolis.* He flipped to the front cover: Franz Fanon. Then back to the sentence, its meaning surging through him like disease. In Iraq, he had been an extension of his city. And if he'd been an extension of the principles of his city, his sister was in the Mayor's office, extending the same thing. *The Church in the colonies is a white man's Church… It does not call the colonized to the ways of God, but to the ways of the white man, to the ways of the master, to the ways of the oppressor. And as we know, in this story many are called but few are chosen.*

He had chosen himself, in the end.

The riot in his brain slowly organized itself, rewriting his life with secret malevolence: Risk pools, systems, moral hazard, the Mexicans he'd looked down on, his own great-grandfather, Herman, suiting up in the U.S. Army uniform to become the colonizer rather than the colonized.

The colonized subject will first train this aggressiveness sedimented in his muscles against his own people. This is the period where black turns on black . . .

All of it was written in fire. And once he knew how to look for it, he found the crackle of oppression everywhere: Walter Scott, Freddie Gray, the Charleston nine. He followed protests, read police reports, made thoughtful denotations of their lying. He knew war and the thoughts of killers. It was his special insight, knowing that. But that was not the most terrifying thing, that he'd for years wished to be the thing that hated him. The most terrifying thing was that he would go back to it, knowing everything. He woke up one afternoon feeling this danger all over him, like a siege. The television blared. It showed the markets closing on CNBC. He didn't know who had turned it to that channel (though of course it had been him, he was the only person there) and Morgan's voice was speaking to him directly through the guests: "The market has its wisdom and if you don't respect the market, it will cut you off at the knees. The market is not about belief. It's not about truth. It's not even about being right. You might be right, but it doesn't matter at all if the market disagrees . . ."

The neighbors called his sister. When she came home, he'd taken the TV outside and shot it—more a symbolic act, to get that voice out of his head, though he knew it looked bad. "Fuck you. Fuck you. There is no fucking way you're getting me back." He may have been saying that out loud to his sister, once she arrived. He may also have had his great-grandfather's pistol in his hand—not much, compared to the weapons he used to command, but still.

"Now I'm going to tell you what you need to do, Ernesto," his sister said from the deck, keeping her back pressed against the door. "Now we're going to stop pretending with each other. I need you to listen carefully to me."

WHITNEY TERRELL'S novel, *The Good Lieutenant* (FSG) was selected as a best book of 2016 by *The Washington Post*, *The Boston Globe,* and *Refinery 29.* It was long-listed for the Andrew Carnegie Medal for Excellence in Fiction. He is also the author of *The Huntsman* and *The King of Kings County*. He was an embedded reporter in Iraq during 2006 and 2010 and covered the war for the *Washington Post Magazine*, *Slate*, and NPR. His nonfiction has additionally appeared in *The New York Times*, *Harper's*, and *The New Republic.* He teaches at the University of Missouri-Kansas City.

HELEN BENEDICT

Snapshots of Hate and Resistance: Charlottesville, VA, August, 2017

A young white man, cheeks as smooth as a toddler's under his Nazi helmet, screams racist rhetoric into the air, his chin and mouth trembling with anger. He looks ready to burst into tears.

Another white man, thin and wiry, paces back and forth in such a frenzy that he keeps hitting his own helmeted head with the pole of his Confederate flag.

A third white man, this one tall and muscular, leans over a police barrier spitting words of white supremacy. Chest thrust out, face red, body straining, he is visibly aching to argue and punch.

"Jews go back to Israel, Asians to Asia..." he yells. "Everyone gets handouts and breaks except the white man!"

A woman built like a bulldog stalks by with her neo-Nazi group, one of only five or so women I saw among the 500 white supremacists present that day. Her middle finger is raised to the surrounding crowd of protesters. She, too, loves this; head up, cheeks flushed with righteousness.

They are all feeding off one another, staying close together under their KKK and Confederate flags, their Nazi symbols, their appropriations of the Stars and Stripes. Their postures and self-satisfied expressions clearly say that they feel, for the moment, pumped with power.

I am taking these verbal snapshots in Charlottesville, Virginia, on the morning of August 12, 2017, at the white nationalist rally that was to shake the country, and expose the president's sympathy with white supremacy more starkly than anything had before. It was also the day that social justice activist, Heather Heyer, was murdered at only thirty-two years old, and that DeAndre Harris was brutally beaten for simply being an American citizen of African descent.

I was there with another writer, Cris Beam. We were staying at a nearby artist's residency just down the road, the Virginia Center for the Creative Arts, and had decided to forego work for a day and head into town. She and I are both journalists, as well as novelists, but we went that day as private citizens to protest white supremacy and bear witness.

There is a difference between covering an event as a journalist and bearing witness as a citizen. A journalist must estimate numbers and gather quotes from all sides, and try to keep her own opinions at bay. A citizen can simply stare. So, what I witnessed that day was something I might never have had time to take in as a journalist: the body language of hate, and conversely, the body language of resistance.

Cris and I were scared. Only the night before, the KKK had marched through the University of Virginia campus, holding torches like a lynch mob. They intimidated ministers praying in a nearby church, and attacked protesting students with the flames of those torches, lighters, and pepper spray. The governor of Virginia told people to stay away on August 12.

So, we decided to avoid the mayhem in the street and instead stand on a grassy slope leading up to Emancipation Park and the statue of Confederate General Robert E. Lee, the flashpoint of the rally. It was the city's plan to remove Lee's statue that had brought white supremacists swarming into Charlottesville from all over the country, ostensibly in protest, but really to flex their muscles, garner publicity—and, it soon became apparent, to fight.

Up on our slope, surrounded by horrified onlookers, black and white, young and old, women and men, we were able to see much of what was going on. We gaped, clutched each other's hands, and gaped some more. Neither of us had ever seen the body language of hate so close up and in such numbers.

Right beside us we saw another disturbing sight: rows of heavily armed militiamen standing along the sides of the road, legs apart, hands gripping automatic rifles, chests bulging with bulletproof vests. They were dressed in a motley collection of military fatigues from various past wars, no doubt bought at their local Army Surplus stores. But their pistols and automatic rifles were current enough. Several of those rifles looked like M4s, the weapon of choice among American soldiers in Iraq.

"Look at the National Guard," someone said.

They were not National Guard. One had blond dreadlocks; many were bearded. Their blouses did not match their pants. Their footwear was all over the place, as were their ages. Some wore helmets, others baseball caps, some were bareheaded. A few had headphones clamped over their ears. At least one wore a bandolier of shotgun shells. Several wore patches simulating the Confederate flag.

But they all had weapons and they were all white, except for one puzzling black man, who hid behind his sunglasses.

Like the white supremacists, these militiamen's faces, too, were set in anger. But even more striking were their expressions of self-importance as they glared at the counter-protesters gathering in the street, and at the Unitarian Universalist ministers singing songs of peace and love only a few feet away, among them Professor Cornel West.

I tried to catch the eyes of these militiamen just to see what was in there. But their eyes were either hidden behind sunglasses, or deliberately avoiding contact.

And then, there were the police. Clad in neon green vests, as if they might be hard to see in the bright sunlight, they stood in rows behind the metal barriers they had erected on both sides of the street. They were far back from the crowds, unreachable.

Cris and I quickly realized we were in a sandwich. In front of us, close enough to touch, were the militiamen, the street, and the amassing neo-Nazis and counter-protesters. Behind us were the police barricaded between gates, and behind them the growing crowd of white nationalists gathering around the statue of Lee, who sat on his bronze horse, blind to what he had wrought.

I kept turning around to watch those police officers, wondering why they weren't responding to the militia, the weapons, the giant cans of pepper spray I saw dangling from neo-Nazi belts. It was as if the police, too, were blind and stuck in place.

Meanwhile, more and more white supremacists were arriving in clumps to wend their way up to the park, chanting their Nazi slogans. The counter-protesters chanted back, "Nazi scum off our streets!"

Then my eye caught a commotion to our left. "Cris, look!" I said, pointing up Main Street. A towering white man with long gray hair, who bore more than a passing resemblance to The Dude in *The Big Lebowski*, was marching down the hill, leading a phalanx of about 100 white supremacists flying Nazi and Confederate flags. Many of them were carrying huge shields painted with various fascist and racist symbols. Many were also wearing helmets and wielding sticks.

At the same time, to our right, the crowd of counter-protesters was approaching, waving signs: "Wake Up and Smell the Nazis," "America Was Built on the Backs of Slaves." And simply, "Wrong 'Hood."

The police stood blinking in the sun.

The Dude led his army with visible aggression, everything about his stride and posture proclaiming he had no intention of giving way to anybody.

The counter-protesters—ministers, women, men, students, young and old—marched on.

The two groups drew closer and closer. The fascists and racists raised their shields and sticks, set their jaws, and chanted Nazi slogans in a mass of male voices: "Blood and soil," and, "You will not replace us/Jews will not replace us."

The counter-protesters, at least half of whom were women, and many of whom were people of color, kept moving forward, waving their signs of peace and resistance.

The police kept on blinking.

As the two flanks moved closer and closer, it was like watching a lit fuse creeping toward a bomb. The police had plenty of time to step between them, form a line, and prevent the mêlée that was clearly coming. But they moved not a muscle.

(Later, the police chief of Charlottesville excused this by saying that the militias and white supremacists had more powerful weapons than the police did.)

At the last moment, a small group of people dressed entirely in black pushed their way to the front of the counter-protesters, carrying a flag saying Antifa. Their faces were masked with scarves. Some had helmets, a few had shields and sticks, some had A for Anarchism patches on their arms. There were 20 of them. They were the only sign I saw of readiness for violence from the counter-protesters, except for a couple of people wearing helmets, clearly expecting to be whacked on the head. One of those helmets read PRESS in wobbly white letters.

By now, the two flanks were face to face. And that is when it happened. Cris and I saw it clearly.

The Dude led the charge. He and the other white supremacists ducked down and rammed right into the counter-protesters, using their shields and sticks and fists to send people flying. Colored smoke billowed. Pepper spray sprayed. Water bottles flew. People screamed and ran.

I turned to an officer behind me. "At what point are you going to do something?" I asked.

His reply: "When the crowd gets out of control."

With the fighting escalating and the tear gas billowing toward us, Cris and I decided to leave. We couldn't. The police had blocked every side road around, hemming us in. All we could do was move further down Main Street.

There, we saw that about seven militiamen had climbed to the roof of a funeral parlor and taken up guard positions; how they got there, I do not know. They had even erected a little tent to protect them from the sun. They crouched, assault rifles in hand, looking down at us unarmed civilians milling unprotected in the streets. Everything about their stance was in imitation of soldiers; exactly as if we were in a war and they were awaiting the order to shoot.

I looked around again for the police to see if they were doing anything about these unofficial snipers. Not an officer in sight.

Time passed. The militia melted away, the last Nazi group marched by, the street began to empty. And then, suddenly, the police appeared after all, an army of them in riot gear forming a black wall across the road. Black clothes, black helmets, masks, guns, huge transparent shields. They stood in formation, like a row of sinister robots.

Nobody was on the street anymore but us, a smattering of counter-protesters, children, and a guy in a kilt carrying a sign saying, "Real Clansmen Wear Kilts."

Who, exactly, we asked each other, were the police protecting here?

But the police, white nationalist and militias were not the only people we saw that day. There was also the resistance.

Earlier that morning, when Cris and I had driven into Charlottesville, we happened across the very church where Cornel West had led an interfaith prayer at sunrise, and where he and a group of ministers—women and men of various ethnic groups and religions, most of them far from young—were gathering to peacefully protest the white nationalist rally.

One woman in her seventies offered us purple cowls to wear if we wished to march with them. "We are ministers and we are trained to be arrested," she told me. "Would you join us?"

Being neither religious nor trained for arrest, I declined. But by chance, Cris and I ended up spending most of our time near them anyway. We found them in front of the park, standing with linked arms, alternately facing front and back, singing "This Little Light of Mine" and other gospel and civil rights anthems. The louder the Nazi chants grew, the more full-throated and melodious rose the preachers' songs.

"Let's stay here," Cris said. "I feel intellectually safer with Cornel West."

At times the ministers knelt, at times they stood, all the while the hate teeming around them, homophobic signs mixing freely with racist and Nazi slogans. An elderly hippie stood nearby, and each time a white supremacist group marched past chanting their words of hate, he rang a bell and banged a tambourine to drown them out. He was surprisingly effective.

Cris and I watched the ministers' faces. Earnest and determined, yes, and sometimes nervous, too, but they wore none of the anger and self-righteousness we saw on the faces of the haters. The difference between an expression of determination and that of antagonism is striking.

We saw several African American reporters and photographers running close alongside the marching white supremacists, taking their pictures and asking questions, despite the verbal abuse being hurled at them and the prominent display of weapons.

We also saw many citizens bearing witness with their phone cameras when the white supremacists attacked.

All around us, I realized, we were seeing resistance in the form of small acts of courage: singing, staring, praying, photographing – some were even trying to engage in a rational discussion with the Nazis. Much of this courage was coming from the citizens of Charlottesville, for the city was not happy with the invasion of these people spouting hate. It is not a home to white supremacy. Not any more. As one young resident proclaimed in outrage, "I've lived in Charlottesville 21 years and I've never seen a white supremacist rally here before. Since Trump was elected, there have been five!"

At one point, Cris and I went to seek a bathroom in a side street restaurant. On the door, the management had hung a sign: "Please leave your weapons outside." Given the open carry law in Virginia, and the horrifying fact that it was legal to bring all those weapons to the rally, this modest sign seemed positively defiant; another act of courage.

On our way out, I saw a waitress writing on the menu board in chalk. Her words:

"What the world needs now,

"Is love, sweet love..."

Two weeks later, I drove back through Charlottesville on my way home to New York. There, I found the streets strewn with flowers and photographs of Heather Heyer. And in the park, now empty of white supremacists, militias, or, indeed, of any people at all, stood Robert E. Lee's statue. Every inch of him was wrapped in black plastic. This proud defender of slavery had at last been shrouded in shame.

HELEN BENEDICT, a professor at Columbia University, has written seven novels, including the recent *Wolf Season*, and *Sand Queen*, a Publishers Weekly "Best Contemporary War Novel." Her journalism inspired the Academy Award-nominated documentary *The Invisible War*, and instigated a landmark lawsuit against the Pentagon on behalf of victims of military sexual assault. A recipient of the Ida B. Wells Award for Bravery in Journalism and the James Aronson Award for Social Justice Journalism, Benedict is also the author of five works of nonfiction, including the book, *The Lonely Soldier: The Private War of Women in Iraq*.

JAMES MATHEWS

Silence All Who Cry Out

"I didn't think you'd show."

"I said I would, didn't I?"

"You said you'd keep in touch too. That was a year ago."

"Do you want me to leave?"

"No. Sit. You look good. Like a good little civie."

"We're all civies now."

"And honorable."

"What's that mean?"

"Nothing. Just that some took to civilian life better than others."

"It's not hard. As long as you understand it's a two-way street."

"What is?"

"Forget it."

"I was thinking that when we saw each other, when you walked up, that we'd share one of those long-lost war buddy hugs."

"You said you didn't think I'd show."

"If you did. If you did, we'd hug it out. Like war buddies do. Like honorable war buddies."

"You really want me to leave, don't you?"

"That's not an option for either of us. Besides, you're already here. You're already sitting."

"Did you order?"

"I told the waiter not to disturb us. I told him I'd call him over if we needed him."

"And what did he think of that?"

"You don't see him around, do you?"

"Let's just get this over with, okay? Say what you've got to say."

"Rules of engagement first."

"Don't fuck around."

"Seriously, you were always the stickler for ROE. With one notable exception. I just want to make sure what we say here is the final word."

"I don't even know what that means."

"That once we start, we finish."

"Fine."

"Because I don't think we're going to get another chance."

"I said fine. Jesus, say what you need to say."

"Balad Theater Hospital, Iraq. POW ward."

"Okay."

"Prisoner 127."

"Okay."

"You know who I'm talking about?"

"I know. You know I know."

"I dream about him. He screams in pain all through the dream. And then he stops."

"Why?"

"You know."

"I know I know. I'm asking you to say it. That's why you wanted to meet, isn't it?"

"He stops because you put a pillow—"

"Someone. *Someone* put a pillow over his face."

"I was there. I was standing right next to you."

"So maybe it was you."

"It wasn't. I was watching the door."

"Doesn't matter. We were there together. Prisoner 127 stopped screaming. He's with his 72 virgins and every American and Brit kid in that hospital got their first good night sleep in days."

"I didn't think it would matter. I was wrong."

"I'm not sure what I can say to you to help you. I never had any dreams about what happened. So I wouldn't know how to stop them. That's what you want, isn't it? A way to stop the dreams."

"Yes."

"Like I said, I don't know what I can do to help."

"I guess I just don't quite understand how you can go on without a second thought about it."

"I never said I didn't think about it."

"But you seem to be doing alright. You got a good job after the army. You got a wife. Maybe even a kid. Do you have a kid?"

"Stay on topic. You want to know why I can handle it and you can't."

"I think so."

"Because Prisoner 127 was going to die anyway. Half his face was gone. He had no arms. He was a hot mess waiting to die. About the only thing he could do was scream and he would have kept on screaming for another three or four days."

"They should have drugged him better."

"They drugged him fine. I was on duty when they pumped him full of all kinds of shit just to get him to shut up. I was there when the doctor called him a 'bad kill' and a waste of pain meds."

"So you put a pillow over his face."

"Someone put a pillow over his face. And somebody else stood by and watched."

"He didn't fight it."

"No, he didn't. That says a lot. So you need to ask yourself how much worse your dreams would be now if you let him live those three or four days."

"I don't know if they'd be worse."

"I don't know either. All I know is that I do think about it every now and then but I also sleep okay."

"I don't."

"Then you need to give it some time."

"How much time?"

"How would I know? Look, I read about this research they did on families whose sons died in the war."

"They?"

"People who research those things. And they found that the first year is the worst, that families can't get over certain images in their minds, of their loved one dying, body all twisted up, shot up, blown up, in agony or whatever. But after a while, two or three years, those images slowly get replaced by nice memories, memories when the person was young and happy. Before the war. Before the army even."

"This is different."

"Of course it is. But not by much."

"I never knew Prisoner 127. I never knew what his face or body looked like before we blew it all apart. I never heard his voice when it wasn't screaming in pain."

"Stop. He was a 'bad kill', nothing more. And *he* blew his own face off. Trying to build a bomb to kill one of your other honorable war buddies probably."

"The doctors. They—"

"The doctors didn't give a shit what happened to him. Do you think they didn't know how he really died? They knew."

"They didn't know."

"Listen to me. They knew. I'm telling you they knew and they didn't care."

"Look at me."

"I am. You look like shit."

"I don't sleep. I fucking live at the VA clinic."

"Does it help?"

"We wouldn't be here if it did. They tell me I need to find the answers by talking it out."

"With them?"

"With you."

"So you tracked me down so we could talk it out and now we've talked it out. I don't know what else there is to say."

"I guess there isn't. I just wanted to know if you felt the same way I do. The fact that you came tells me maybe you do. Maybe you hear the screams when you're awake and I just hear them when I sleep."

"I'm leaving."

"Back to your wife? Your kid?"

"Stick with the VA. Things will get better. In two or three years, you'll remember it all very differently."

"I'll have happy thoughts about Prisoner 127?"

"I never said that. Take care of yourself."

"Seriously, will I even be here in two or three years?"

"Don't try to put that shit on me."

"Will I have to be silenced? Will the doctors know how I died? Will they care?"

"I can't help you, man. You have to help yourself."

"A two-way street?"

"Sure."

"I'm going to try. I'm going to look for those happy memories."

"Or just different ones. Settle for that."

"Like you?"

"Sure. Like me. Just like me."

JAMES MATHEWS grew up in El Paso, Texas and now lives in Maryland. His stories have appeared in numerous literary journals, including *Painted Bride Quarterly, The Pacific Review, Carolina Quarterly, The Florida Review, Northwest Review*, and many more. His short story collection, *Last Known Position*, received the 2008 Katherine Anne Porter Prize in Short Fiction and was published by the University of North Texas Press. He is also a retired Air Force/Air National Guard Chief Master Sergeant who has served overseas numerous times, including two tours in Iraq (in 2003 and 2006). His website is www.jamesmathewsonline.com.

www.ingramcontent.com/pod-product-compliance
Lightning Source LLC
Chambersburg PA
CBHW050037040726
47599CB00015B/1723

* 9 7 8 0 6 9 2 0 6 5 4 6 4 *